THE COVERT SPIRIT OF OFFENSE

APOSTLE DANNIE WILLIAMS

This edition first published 2026

Library of Congress Cataloging-in-Publication Data
Williams, Dannie
The Covert Spirit of Offense, Dannie Williams
p. cm.- (publishing info here)

ISBN: 979-8-234-03701-5 (paperback: alk, paper)

FOREWORD

By Pastor Brenda Ray

Redemptive Life Palm Beach

Offense is one of the most underestimated forces shaping the lives of believers today. It hides quietly, grows subtly, and spreads rapidly. In this book, Apostle Dannie Williams confronts this reality with clarity, conviction, and pastoral honesty. He exposes offense not as a momentary irritation but as a spiritual strategy designed to derail purpose, fracture relationships, and weaken the effectiveness of the church.

What makes this work important is its practicality. Apostle Williams does not simply diagnose the problem; he walks the reader through the internal patterns, biblical examples, and emotional cycles that allow offense to take root. His teaching is direct but compassionate, challenging readers to examine themselves without shame and to pursue healing without delay. Through the stories of Cain, Saul, David, and others, he shows how offense can distort perception, corrupt motives, and ultimately destroy destiny if left unaddressed.

This book is not written to expose others but to illuminate the hidden places within us. It calls every believer to maturity, honesty, and spiritual responsibility. It reminds us that breakthrough is not only a matter of faith but also of the condition of the heart. The message is simple but urgent: offense must be confronted, or it will control us.

Readers will find this book both sobering and liberating. It offers a path toward emotional wholeness, spiritual clarity, and healthier relationships. Most importantly, it points us back to the character of Christ, who showed us what it means to forgive, to release, and to live free.

This work is timely, necessary, and deeply relevant for anyone seeking to grow in God and walk in true spiritual freedom.

ACKNOWLEDGMENTS

The greatest teachers in our lives are oftentimes not found in classrooms, but in the experiences that impact our lives. I want to thank all my wonderful teachers who helped me to write this book.

'Thank you' to the most important and incredible women in my life: my wonderful wife and friend, Dr. Precious, and my daughters, Danae', Danisha and Seles. All of you taught me more than I could ever imagine and even more than I will ever know. You are the greatest cheerleading squad any winner could ask for.

To the ministry leaders of Citadel of Hope: 'Thank you'. All of you taught me that it is okay to grow while you see others grow. I shall always love you for all you are to me, but most of all, for allowing me to be the teacher and the pupil at the same time.

Thanks to all my spiritual sons and daughters of Kingdom Covenant Fellowship, partners, members, and friends. All of you taught me that it is a wonder for children to see the flaws of a father, but serve him as if none existed. The relationships you have allowed me to have with all of you may have empowered you, but they energized me.

Finally, 'thank you' to all who taught me the grace of perseverance and gave me the drive to survive.

Winning is the ability to learn wisdom from every experience.

TABLE OF CONTENTS

***

***

CHAPTER ONE

The Spirit of Offense: *The Covert Operation*

Your faith won't move God if you have issues in your lives that you need to deal with. What is happening to a lot of people in the body of Christ is that they are trying to access things in the Spirit realm that they don't have legal authority to access, and when they don't get them, they become frustrated and discouraged. They want to blame God, the church, people in their family, or anyone else, because they are praying and attempting to have faith for things that they are not in a spiritual position to receive. We need to find out what is hindering the body of Christ from experiencing all that God has ordained for us and what is preventing our faith from manifesting the fullness of its potential.

The Spirit of God revealed to me a powerful truth as to why many in the body of Christ's prayers are not being answered, and why their faith is not working. Here is the truth that the Spirit of God showed me: the biggest hindrance to the body of Christ not walking in victory and not getting breakthroughs is due to the ***spirit of offense***.

There are many levels and characteristics of the ***spirit of offense***, and many manifestations of it.

You must be honest while you are reading this book. Whenever the Spirit of God speaks to you, just put a star by that note and say, "That's me." Many people who read this book are instigators of some type of offense, or they are dealing with the result of some type of offense. They have no clue that it is an offense that is delaying their promises, breakthroughs, and healings.

***

I was meditating one day, and the Spirit of God showed me a vision of an octopus. In this vision, the octopus had a big head, and connected to the head were eight tentacles. The Lord informed me that the ***spirit of offense*** is the head, and the tentacles represent anger, discord, rebellion, distrust, division, infirmity, mental or emotional imbalance, and unforgiveness. These tentacles or issues most often can be traced back to some offense that the person has not gotten victory over or confronted. It has to be frustrating for us to fast, pray, and hear the word of God and still not see the growth in God we so desperately need or desire. It must be even more frustrating to come out of a powerful worship service and still struggle with personal issues, with no idea that God wants to change our lives. Many times, there is an offense there that, as Christians, we do not want to recognize.

The greatest levels of spiritual maturity are always found in our inability to diagnose ourselves and to recognize that there are some offenses in our hearts or lives.

> ***The heart knows his own bitterness.***
>
> ***-Proverbs 14:10, KJV***

We tend to go through stuff, but we don't work through stuff.

When you go through a difficult situation or have an offensive experience, some people will tell you don't worry about it, just forget it or they may get really deep and tell you that you simply need to get your praise on. All that is good and has its place, but there still comes a time in life when you need to slow down long enough and **process the process**. Still, we tend to, as Christians, go through stuff, but we don't work through it. An offense may happen today, and then a week passes. In the next month or year, it happens again, and we think it's over, but the offense is still somewhere in your soul until you confront it and deal with it. If you had a job working in an environment where you are breathing chemicals that are harmful to you, just because you quit the job, does not mean that the effects of your working there are over. There are statistics of military men and women who are suffering from Post-Traumatic Stress Disorder (PTSD) today as a result of being involved in military conflicts from years ago.

Just because the offensive act is over, it does not mean that the effect of the offense is over.

For this cause many are weak and sickly among you, and many sleep.

-I Corinthians 11:30, KJV

The Corinthians had not come to a place where they completely understood the importance of having a pure heart towards God and towards each other. We need to understand why we're responding as we do. When we hear certain things, when we go through certain situations, when people say certain things to us or about us, why does it really shake us? We are supposed to be mature enough in Christ that certain things don't bother us. We are supposed to be dead in Christ until certain things don't shake us. Offenses will keep rattling our lives as long as we are connected to the offenses.

What you do not master will master you.

It will ultimately seize your mind, your soul, your body, and possibly your spirit, and literally take you on a journey that you will not enjoy or cause you to not enjoy life and experience your best life.

****

THE FIVE LEVELS LEADING TO THE SPIRIT OF OFFENSE:

Let us look at the different levels of events that lead to the ultimate level of living with the ***spirit of offense***.

1. **THE REGRET LEVEL:** This is the level where the incident is not of a major consequence. This is

something that we wish had not happened, but it happened, and it's no big deal.

2. **THE DISAPPOINTMENT LEVEL:** At this level, you knew this was going to hurt, but you allowed it anyway. It is not life-threatening, and it is not destructive, but it lingers on your mind, and you just can't shake it.

3. **THE HURT LEVEL:** This level is attached to a principle. It's not what was done, but it's the principle behind it. The idea of what was done is not as major as the motivation behind why it was done. At this level, the emphasis is on principle and not incident. There is a difference between an incident and a principle.

   A. Incident - This is a single situation, with minor consequences or levels of offenses. How do you handle an incident? Talk about it and resolve it. **Remember, when it's over, it's over.**

B. Principle - This is a situation steeped in principle. If you don't address the principle, chances are the situation will be repeated repeatedly. Someone saying 'Sorry' is not going to fix it. You must sit down and painstakingly look at the principle with resolutions as the objective.

4. **THE OFFENSE LEVEL:** This is the yellow warning light level. At this level, you get to the point that you don't trust anything that the person who offended you says. You find it difficult to trust the person, or who the person represents, because you have been through so many hurts with that person, or someone who resembles that person.
5. **THE SPIRIT OF OFFENSE LEVEL:** This level is beyond a talking session. This level has reached massive life control. Any person constantly hitting walls, running into misunderstandings, and overreacting to incidents, situations, and circumstances in life has reached this level. At this level, there is the constant manifestation of the tentacles of the octopus. The ***spirit of offense*** has

not been dealt with, and, therefore, it intensifies as the years go by. This is a level that requires major spiritual intervention.

That you may approve things that are excellent,

that ye may be sincere and without offense till the day of Christ.

-Philippians 1:10, KJV

Paul lets us know that to participate in the promise and grace God has promised, your life is going to have to be a lifestyle of excellence. If your life is going to be a lifestyle of excellence, you've got to be sure you are sincere and without offense. If you have offense in your life, your life cannot be excellent, and if your life is not excellent, you cannot partake of God's good grace.

The issue is not that God does not want to bless or help us; the issue is that there is something between what God wants to do for us and where we are, and it's the spirit of offense.

Until the day that Christ appears, you and I are supposed to constantly live our lives without offense. The word of God teaches us that offenses are going to happen to all of us. We are not like we are because of things that happen to us; we are like we are because we have not resolved the things that happened to us. If going through is the justification for us being like we are, then all of us ought to be messed up and offended, because all of us have been through something.

Some people have been through very horrible situations, broken relationships, abuses, etc., and their response has been different than the response of others who went through the same things. Some have decided not to let bad situations control their personality or the rest of their lives. You and I could spend the rest of our lives constantly blaming yesterday for how we are today, and live with the spirit of fear to the point that we will never get a breakthrough. If we do, we will never step into what God wants for our lives. We could spend all our lives just going around in circles, just hoping and praying that one day we get off the merry-go-round. Still, there comes a time in your life when you must decide that enough is enough. You must decide that I am not going to be offended. You must decide that even if others were offended, and others don't respect anybody, and others told everybody how they felt, and even if your daddy was a rolling stone, or what your mother did, and what your aunt did, and what your uncle did—you have to decide that you're going to a be a solitary in the family and that you are going to show everybody else what it means to live an offense-free life. You can't live the rest of your days controlled by what happened to you yesterday. God wants to break the ***spirit of offense*** that's keeping the body of Christ from its full inheritance. Paul says we are supposed to be sincere and without offense until the day of Christ.

These things have I spoken unto you that you should not be offended

-St. John 16:1, KJV

So, we know that it is not the will of God for us to walk around offended. It is not the will of God for us to have a confession of, "Well, you know, I've just got some unresolved issues." Let's resolve the issues, kill the octopus, and go on to destiny. Getting healed and getting whole is a lot of self-work, not the church work, and not church leadership work. Getting healed, healthy, and whole is a lot of self-work, meaning you must go to God with his word, and you must constantly work on yourself. I am talking about praying and letting the Father know, "Father, this is me. This is how I am, and I know the way I am is not pleasing you."

They shall put you out of the synagogue

-St. John 16:2, KJV

You might ask the question, "Am I not supposed to be offended when I am offended, even in church? What if they kill me and think they are doing the will of God?" You are not supposed to be offended when people are talking about you and trying to kill your character and integrity. I am talking about taking on the nature of Christ. Jesus is teaching you what's going to happen, so that you won't be surprised when it happens, because he doesn't want you to be offended when it happens. When they kill you (talk about you), they think that they are doing the will of God, but don't get offended. You are supposed to look right at your offenders just as Jesus did at those who were crucifying him and said to them, **"Father, forgive them."** When Jesus forgave them, it demonstrated to us the power to forgive our offenders.

I believe that had Jesus allowed offense to get into His heart and then been taken off the cross and put in the tomb, when He would have tried to go through hell with offense in His heart, Jesus would have gotten stuck in hell. When He said, **"Father, forgive them,"** He was really releasing from Him the debt of their offense and not just forgiving them for what they did. Because when you forgive, it has more to do with you than them. In other words, you are not just releasing them from what they did, you are releasing yourself. Forgiveness is not about making the other person feel good, but it is about making yourself feel better about the fact that you are going to need God to forgive you one day.

One of the major lessons that I have learned is that I cannot afford to hold unforgiveness against anyone. Being offended is too costly!

We can be selfish in forgiveness, realizing that the greatest benefactor of forgiveness is the person who forgives. The fact of the matter is that we wouldn't forgive if God didn't tell us that we have to forgive before we can be blessed. If some people could hate others and still make it to heaven, they would.

Jesus tells us in His Word that we are going to be persecuted. Bad things are going to happen to all of us. When bad things happen to us, and we have unresolved offenses, the pain of those issues will connect and form holes in our souls. Offense is the result of an incident or series of incidents that attacks or attaches to a pre-existing hole in one's soul. In other words, there is a hole, an unresolved issue, something that is in your soul that you have not dealt with or resolved.

For years, as a Pastor, I conducted the funerals of members, and they affected me drastically. When church members would pass, their families would call me to see how I was doing because there was a hole in my soul relative to my own parents' passing that I had never completely dealt with. So, every time somebody passed, the pain of it attached itself to the hole that was in my soul. The Spirit of God spoke to me and said if I didn't deal with this, every time someone dies, a piece of me would die. I had to confront that issue, and it was very painful. I didn't like doing but I had to cry to God and do whatever I had to do, but I had to close up the hole that was in my soul. You cannot go around with holes in your soul, because when things happen to you, those things will get inside your soul.

There may be holes in your soul from the time you were a little girl, a teenage boy, a young adult, or a time when something happened to you contrary to your choice. Things that happened in your life, and because you just went through it and never worked through it, when something happens, it's like you have flashbacks, time picks you up and throws you right back in that situation, you relive the moment and the circumstance all over again, and you keep repeating the vicious cycle. God wants to bring you to a place where you can close that hole in your soul, so that you can go to your next level in God. The vicious cycle has got to stop, and it has to stop now!

I know what it is to have a hole in your soul and not deal with it. As a little child, there were people that I knew who said some very negative things about me. Those things became a part of my mental, emotional, and spiritual make-up. Some of us are living out what was told to us or said to us years ago. Those things that were said never seemed to get out of my spirit until I came to a place one day when I decided that I am not going to let this control the rest of my life.

Blessed is he whosoever shall not be offended in Me

-Luke 7:23, KJV

You are blessed when you are not offended, and your life is in Him. There is something wrong with Christians who have the life and power of Christ and are still offended when the nature and the emotion of Christ are supposed to be in us. If we are in Him and He is in us, then all that is like Him is in us. If I am in Christ, my life is hidden with Christ in God.

The prince of this world cometh, but he finds nothing in me

-John 14:30, KJV

You may have been born out of wedlock, but if you are truly a child of the Kingdom, the devil still has nothing in you. They called Jesus Beelzebub, a winebibber and a blasphemer, but the devil had nothing in Him. They wanted to stone Him, and they threw Him out of the synagogue. He came to His own and his own did not receive Him, yet He was able to stand up and say, 'The prince of this world cometh and he finds nothing in me that belongs to him', (John 14:30, KJV). With everything Jesus went through, the devil couldn't put anything in him or take anything out of him. The devil couldn't do it. Jesus was too full of God to be full of the devil. That's the place where God wants to take the body of Christ—a place where we are so full of God that there is no place for the devil in us.

You may have been abused, rejected, disappointed, or the like, and you must recognize your offense, get healed of it, and tell the devil he has had his last day to play on the playground of your mind. Don't get depressed every time you hear the words abuse, rejection, disappointment, or any other negative emotion. Decide and declare that you are not going to let offense control you. Decree that you are so confident in who you are in God that the enemy has no place in you. I have discovered that when things start getting inside my spirit, it is because I was not in complete fellowship and communion with the Spirit of God. When God is in you, and He is the hope of glory that dwells in you, the Bible lets us know we can conquer anything.

This also affects how I live. If I am going to be happy, if I am going to live a stress-free life, I need to live offense-free. Do you understand that people are dropping dead every day from stress? Haven't you noticed that even young people are having heart attacks and falling out? Something crazy is happening all around the world. Don't you know you cannot afford to carry yesterday and today at the same time? Jesus said today has enough evil, sufficient thereof. Enough is going on today, and still, some are carrying today from yesterday!

And have no root in themselves, and so endure but for a time: afterward, when affliction or persecution arises for the word's sake, immediately they are offended

-Mark 4:17, KJV

This teaches us that offended people are oftentimes offended by the word of God. When the word of God is preached or taught, some may hear it, but they do not allow it to change them because the word of God will be tried by the persecution of life. When you hear the word of God, the enemy's objective is to try you, not because you are so great and special, but to try you because of what you just heard. Offenses come to try the word of God that you have been hearing. Jesus described a reality that when they heard the word, tribulation and persecution came, and they got offended. The word of God causes many people to get offended.

The spirit of offense must be broken. It must be dealt with as a very dangerous foe!

It's keeping people back from what God has for them. It's holding them hostage. Some are even sick because of the ***spirit of offense***. The ***spirit of offense*** has convinced some people, when the word is being taught, that they are being attacked. The enemy of offense attacks them by saying, "You don't like this word." Your flesh says, "This is getting on my nerves, this is aggravating me, or this is making me mad." Still, your spirit man says, "Thank you, I want to be free! Thank you, I want to be delivered! Thank you, I need help!" That's when you understand that your spirit is growing and your flesh is dying. When your spirit wants to hear the things of God, your flesh will make every excuse while you are listening to the word. You begin to think, *I need to go to the restroom, I'm getting tired, I'm getting sleepy, I got to go home and take a nap, I need to eat something to take my medication or put this book down and come back to it later.* That's your flesh, but your spirit is saying, 'I don't want these chains on me anymore. I don't want these handcuffs on my hands and these weights on my mind. I want to lay aside every weight that so easily beset me, because I want to fulfill my destiny'.

And then shall many be offended, and shall betray one another, and shall hate one another

-Matthew 24:10, KJV

Offense leads to betrayal and ultimately hatred. It doesn't just remain in one category of your life, but it grows continually. Before you know it, you will be wondering how your life got like this. The Bible says that in the last days, the love of many shall wax cold. The love of many shall wax cold, because offense is going to abound richly. Offenses in the house of God mean that love is going to decline. So many people go to the same church, raise their hands to worship God, but hate each other. If I am offended with you, then I choose to believe the worst about you before I believe the best about you. If I am a married and offended woman, then I choose to believe my husband will cheat on me. If my unsaved, divorced, five-times girlfriend tells me that my husband is no good, even if he is saved, because I am offended, I am going to believe her before I believe the relationship my husband and I have together.

The enemy wants us to betray each other's trust, confidence and loyalty.

There appears to be a stronger covenant in some gangs than there is in some families and churches. You hardly ever hear of gang members who would betray other gang members. This is because they live by a code of commitment that says if one is guilty, all are guilty. The ***spirit of offense*** has to be broken so that we can walk in real love. When people know that you love them, they wouldn't have to say, "Yeah, right. I can't feel it." People are very sensitive these days, and the saints' discernment is getting sharper now. We have got to be real with each other, and certainly in the house of God. There is too much drama and too much offense going on in many of our lives and in the house of God. The only place you find drama is when you find the existence of offenses. People walking in love don't have the time or energy for offenses. We realize that life is too short, we have too much that we are believing God for, we have unsaved family members, we have needs in our lives, and we have situations that we have got to trust God to work out. We don't have time to be offended, not speak to each other, be superficial, and hypocritical. God sees our hearts, and He sees our spirits. We might get over on another person, but we will never get over on God.

> ***A brother offended is harder to be won than a strong city; and their contentions are like the bars of a castle***
>
> ***-Proverbs 18:19, KJV***

When there is a ***spirit of offense***, it is very difficult to resolve the smallest of misunderstandings or disagreements. When you refuse reconciliation, you open your life to a possible invasion of a ***spirit of offense***. One day, it's one person you are offended with, the next day it's two. The next day, it's the whole family, ministry, and the list becomes endless. Now, you don't like anybody, anywhere, at any time. Before you know it, you are saying no one is real or right but you and your perception. Once you get this in your mind, you are offended, and a ***spirit of offense*** has set in, and reasoning goes out the door. There is no acceptable compromise. There is nothing to talk about; nothing said will change your mind. That's a dangerous state of mind. The word of God teaches us that if there is an offense between us, we are supposed to talk and resolve the matter without going to everybody in the church, family, and town.

When one deals with offended people, remember this: fools rush in where angels dare to tread. You should never come to a place in your life where you can't work out offenses.

Forgiveness does not mean that we have to be best buddies afterwards, but saying that you will never trust again is foolish. Contentions are like the bars of a castle in that, when the offended put bars up, no one can reach them. Some people are so offended that they appear to be unreachable because of the offense they are carrying. The tragic thing is that you waited until you got into someone's life before you exploded. Now, emotional shrapnel is all over the place. Many are the wounded dead in relationship with blown up people. There is a different spirit in relationships now. In the old days, people tolerated you. People today will tell you quickly that I am just as crazy as you are. They want to take out all their stress on someone anyway.

We cannot heal what's wrong with you if we don't know what is wrong with you.

We are going to get rid of the ***spirit of offense*** in our marriages, in the body of Christ, and between leadership because the ***spirit of offense*** has got us sick, angry, bitter, and looking old before our time.

The Offense Tool Sheet

Date: ____________________

Time:____________________

***

What did I learn about myself today?

____
____
____
____
____
____

What did the Holy Spirit say to me today?

____
____
____
____
____
____

What victory did I gain today?

____
____
____
____
____

What is my goal to be a better me?

____
____
____

How will I handle not being offended in the future?

How will I handle not offending others?

What are my plans to not participate in others' offense?

Who am I praying for that's offended?

CHAPTER TWO

THE SPIRIT OF OFFENSE: *EXPOSING THE OCTOPUS*

The purpose or motivation for this book is not for you or me to point fingers at everyone who does something wrong or says that they have a ***spirit of offense***. It is for the purpose of recognizing when we ourselves have stepped across the line. The ***spirit of offense*** can be likened to drinking and driving. The thing is, you don't know when you've drunk too much and stepped across the line, and could end up driving drunk. All you know are the ramifications that show up when you've stepped across the line: you get a ticket, pass out at a light, or cause an accident. Taking a drink for the first time does not make someone an alcoholic, but a continuation of that lifestyle could ultimately push them across the line, and they cannot tell which drink made them an alcoholic. It is the same way when it comes to an offense that happens to us; the things that we don't resolve, deal with, confront, expose, or bring healing to could, somewhere along the way, cause us to step across the line, causing a hole in our soul, and it's called a ***spirit of offense***. We then find ourselves in the position of having to recognize the ***spirit of offense***, needing to be delivered, and needing to be made whole in this area of our lives. The Spirit of the Lord shared with me that one of the greatest hindrances to the body of Christ getting breakthroughs in their lives is in the area of **offense**.

There are offended Christians claiming to be in the kingdom of God, but the enemy has caused many of us to paint over our offense and call it by different names. We call it issues, personality traits, or we proudly confess that we just don't take anything from anyone. No! The truth of the matter is that somewhere along your life's journey, you stepped across the line, and a ***spirit of offense*** is now operating in and through you. We need to understand the seriousness of dealing with this as individuals. This is not about me pointing at you or you pointing at me, but being mature enough to look into the mirror of our own souls and say, "I have a problem." We need to be able to say, "God, I need you to minister to this area of my life. God, I need you to put your finger on what's really going on here." No one can help you; even God won't help you if you are not honest and let Him help you.

I want to share with you what God thinks about us when we allow offenses to saturate and settle in our souls. Too often, we allow the issues and circumstances of life to somehow leave their mark and their impact on us. We get older, and all of a sudden, things start happening to our bodies and our minds. *Could this be the harvest from offenses that've been rooted in our souls for years?* We need to know that there is an answer to the hurt that's going on in our lives.

That you may approve things that are excellent, that ye may be sincere and without offense till the day of Christ.

-Philippians 1:10, KJV

Paul says that his desire for us is that we are approved and that we endeavor to be excellent in all things (Philippians 1:10, KJV). Then he goes on to say that we should have sincerity in our lives and that we should be without offense. We see from the word of God that it is possible to live without offense. It is possible to go through things and not come out with a ***spirit of offense***. This is one of the highest goals that you ought to be striving for in your life. God will allow you to go through situations where you will get hit, but you will not get hurt. That's when you know you are victorious.

The ***spirit of offense*** **can be styled as an octopus**. An octopus has the ability to re-grow its tentacles. The way you get rid of an octopus is not to cut its tentacles off, but to cut off its head instead. If you realize you have anger and you get an appointment with a pastor and he counsels you about your anger matter, ask yourself, *have I dealt with rebellion, infirmities, or other issues as a result of offense?* What we have been doing is helping to get rid of one tentacle. You get over anger for a while and move on to concentrating on something else in your life, but while concentrating on that, anger is growing back. In this case, the issue is not just anger; the issue is the ***spirit of offense*** that gives birth to anger. Anger, rebellion, and the like are only symptoms. The ***spirit of offense*** is the cause. The ***spirit of offense*** has no limitations. It destroys relationships, health, mental well-being, and whatever else it can get its hands on.

The octopus does not kill its victims by fighting; it has poison in its tentacles. When the octopus called offense gets its tentacles wrapped around you, the poison from those **tentacles** paralyzes you. What the ***spirit of offense*** does is poison you to the point you cannot be healthy and whole. What are we going to do with this? I am finding in all spheres of life, people are being confronted and exposed to the fact that they must get over their hurt before they can be healed.

A brother offended is harder to be won than a strong city; and their contentions are like the bars of a castle.

-Proverbs 18:19, KJV

When you become an offended Christian, it is very challenging. Proverbs says it is easier to get along with people in the world who are angry than to get along with Christians who are offended. We are not supposed to be like that.

The Gospel of Mark teaches the process of working faith. In it, Jesus says to remember that when you are standing and praying, and you realize that there is an ought between you and your brother, you need to go and be reconciled; this must occur before your faith can work. This is not so much because of your brother, but so that your faith can work. Your faith cannot work when there is offense in your heart. When you carry offense, you can have numerous prophecies in one service, and none of those prophecies will manifest. You then struggle with your reality as to why things are not breaking in your life. Maybe there is an offense there, or maybe you should ask yourself, *Why can't I get out of this rut? Something is going on because the principles of the word of God work!*

We are after the head of the octopus! If you get over offense, you can get over anger, rebellion, infirmity, and the rest. There are some things we have been praying about for the longest time that we need to get healed and delivered from. If you are carrying offenses, you cut yourself off from God's help. You may have prayed so many times and not delivered yet.

Why?

It's because you have been confronting the tentacles and not cutting off the head of the octopus! Something is in you that you won't let go of. Not all offenses are born out of somebody doing you wrong. Some offenses arise out of a lack of expectations being fulfilled in your life.

***

Hope deferred maketh the heart sick.

-Proverbs 13:12, KJV

Why keep on hoping, and it doesn't happen? Proverbs 13:12 says it makes the heart sick, and perhaps that's why time can be such a faith-destroyer, because when it does not happen quickly, your hope is weakened. You might say, "God's going to make a way, God's going to do this for me, and God's going to open a door for me!" and when it does not happen, it makes the heart sick. At some point, you find yourself walking around with offenses in your heart against God. You prayed, and God didn't come through. You believed God, and it didn't work out. You had faith for a relationship with this person, and they hooked up with someone else. We do a lot of things ignorantly and without a scriptural basis. We then try to make God conform to our ignorance and blame him for not manifesting.

One of the things offenses do is hold up breakthroughs and revival in your life. Don't sit around and not fast because you refuse to give up your offenses. Deal with it so that you can get everything God has for your life.

I will go and return to my place, till they acknowledge their offense and seek my face; in their affliction, they will seek me early.

-Hosea 5:15, KJV

The Word says in the book of Hosea, "I am leaving you, until you realize that you have an offense." He says that it is your offense that is going to bring about affliction that's going to drive you back to Him.

Come, and let us return unto the Lord; for he ….

Hosea 6:1, KJV

A lot of things we have been praying for have not manifested. What God is saying is that this is not the kind of environment He wants his presence to exist in. He doesn't want to dwell in an environment where you can't get along with people, you are carrying hurts, you are still carrying the mark of the issues of the things that happened to you, and you will not deal with them.

This is because we tend to go through situations and won't work through situations. We must slow down in life to find out what it is doing to us and how to get better and get over it. Offended people are raising offended children. The word of God says He is leaving and going back on high—until you acknowledge your offenses. When offenses grip your soul, the last person who wants to *acknowledge* that there is something wrong with them is the person who *has* something wrong with them. Don't spend all your life blaming other folks, ***but that doesn't mean that if people do bad things to you, it's your fault.***

What I am saying is this: if you get hurt, you need to get healed, you need to get whole, and you need to get to a point that you don't let people wound or violate you anymore. If you don't get a revelation of this, five years from now, we will visit you somewhere after you have crashed. If they have hurt you, confront and talk about it. If there is an issue and it can be resolved, do so! There is no need to be a super-Christian.

Don't stay on the path to a crash.

The second thing about offense is that people who are offended will try to get you out of your purpose.

But He turned and said unto Peter get thee behind me, Satan: thou art an offense unto me....

-Matthew 16:23, KJV

Perhaps the Apostle Peter had this issue. Offense does not always show up as a negative thing that happens; it arises when an expectation is not manifested. Peter was getting ready to set himself, but Jesus recognized something impure about Peter in one stance. Jesus recognized that Peter had become an offense, to the point that Peter was trying to get Jesus out of his purpose.

Many of us could be a lot further in life if we had not gotten offended or tied up with offended people. Don't get caught up in offense or offended people and get off purpose. Also, if you are single and thinking about getting married, please tell the person everything you are struggling with. It's not fair for your partner to have spent ten years dealing with unresolved offenses before they can enjoy the marriage.

Many of us are supposed to be so far in the kingdom, but we were slowed down because we did what Abraham did: we took a Lot along with us. The word of

God teaches us that after Lot left, it was then that the Lord took Abraham out and showed him the stars, representing his promise and potential. There are some people we allow in our lives that we need to be open and honest with, so both parties in the relationship will have and live healthy, whole lives. Ultimately, even with all the preaching, worshipping, praying, prophesying, five-fold ministry gifts, and all these other gifts in the body of Christ, something is still not clicking. The word of God should be made manifest in our lives. God has blessings in store for us, but until we acknowledge the offenses, He is going back up to the high place, per the Prophet Hosea.

Woe unto the world because of offenses! For it must needs be that offenses come; but woe to that man by whom the offense cometh.

-Matthew 18:7, KJV

Offended people are self-destructive people.

When you carry offenses, the only person you end up destroying is you. You are not hurting or harming anyone, as much as you are hurting yourself. You may feel like you can tell people off, feel like you can do what you want to do, and say whatever you want to about folks, but at the end of it all, the only person who will ultimately be destroyed is you. I once listened to a woman talk about anger and what it did to her after her son was stabbed and died. She did not know how to let go of the anger over his death. She talked about how the anger got so bad that it destroyed her family, even though her family had nothing to do with it. Someone else was involved in the son's death, but she couldn't let go of the anger. She was carrying it, and it destroyed her and her family.

You won't do anything to save yourself until you care enough about yourself! Again, we have a habit of going through things, but not working through them. What I am teaching in this book is going to require work. It's easy to go to a beauty shop and get another hairstyle, go to the store and buy another dress, go get a haircut, or get another suit; that is just dealing with the exterior.

The ***spirit of offense*** is like a poisonous octopus with all its tentacles wrapped around different parts of your life. Just when you think you have pulled away one part of it, here comes something else, and you have to keep going until the head dies. All of it must die! One of the methods to deal with offense is to CRY: Confront-Repent-Yield. We will expand on this in the worksheet section.

Something that makes us defensive and want to get people back who hurt us is pride. The Word teaches us that Jesus, having no reputation, humbled Himself. This means that Jesus was not concerned about what the angels in heaven or the demons in hell thought about Him. He was only concerned about obeying the Father. So, He made for himself no reputation. Understand that it is not about you, but you must know and fully realize your purpose and assignment in life. We are living in an environment with a lot of hurt people, and hurt people hurt people. Some people get triggered easily. Something sets them off, and they are not easily agreeable, which causes contention. It's as if poison is in their soul.

Offended people are often the greatest instigators of witchcraft. They attempt to control you with their offense. They are offended, and although there are some things you want to say to them, their offenses control you so that you don't say to them what they need to be told, because you are afraid you might set them off. Some of us needed to have been set straight years ago. We don't help people by enabling them to continue in offense. Help them, when possible, by telling them that they are carrying a ***spirit of offense***.

When you get ready to see yourself, then God can help you.

If somebody had told me that I was carrying some things that the Lord had to break off me over the past few years, I would have been a lot further in life. When God starts using people to tell you their story, it's because you need to be told about yourself. You can walk around still harboring negative feelings about deceased individuals, and they could be in heaven or hell based on their choices. Now, what are you going to do with the rest of your life? "Well, someone touched me the wrong way." How long are you going to go on with that? How long will you use yesterday's crutch for today's excuse?

We go through things, but we don't work through things.

Offense will have you running around and around in circles until you decide that enough is enough.

And herein do I exercise myself, to have always a conscious

void of offense toward God, and toward men

-Acts 24:16, KJV

You could feel like you are offended by God. God does not want us worshipping, clapping our hands, and praising Him because we are scared that we are going to hell. He wants us to do those things because we love Him. He says we need to have a conscience void of offense. There should be nothing offensive between my God and any other relationships, including my brothers and sisters in the Lord. We must not have nor tolerate a ***spirit of offense***. Right now, you ought to say, "After reading this book, I will not lie down tonight with anything in my heart against anyone. I am choking these tentacles one by one, and then I am going to kill the head. I am not stopping until the ***spirit of offense*** is dead."

Giving no offense in anything that the ministry be not blamed.

-II Corinthians 6:3, KJV

Paul lets us know that Christians are not to have offenses to the point that unbelievers are talking about the church in the world. We are supposed to be in an environment where when people walk into worship environments, they feel the love of God. If there are disagreements, there is a scriptural way we are to handle them. Still, when you are offended, you are not going to do things the scriptural way. Your carnality and flesh will cause you to act inappropriately. The word of God says if you have an ought against your brother, you go right to him and straighten it out. It's between the two of you—not your clique, your buddies, or everyone else. If you are already offended, you are going to simply use the incident as a match, because the fuel was already in you, prepared to explode. That's what's happening inside your soul. The language of the offended is often, '*I don't have anything against anyone, but I just don't like the way I was treated or disrespected*'. The offended will not prosper in God talking like that.

They are not going anywhere in God, and they are certainly not impressing God. The offended should not go into the house of the Lord waving their hands and talking about how much they love God and that God is their everything, when right behind the veil of their mouth is a ***spirit of offense*** where God's glory will not reign, because it does not possess the heart of God. The heart of God is when things happen, so let's heal it and move on.

The Offense Tool Sheet

Date: ____________________

Time: ____________________

***

What did I learn about myself today?

____

____

____

____

____

What did the Holy Spirit say to me today?

____

____

____

____

____

What victory did I gain today?

____

____

____

____

____

What is my goal to be a better me?

____

____

____

How will I handle not being offended in the future?

How will I handle not offending others?

What are my plans to not participate in others' offense?

Who am I praying for that's offended?

CHAPTER THREE

THE SPIRIT OF OFFENSE: *THE COVERT ON CAIN*

That you may approve things that are excellent, that ye may be sincere and without offense till the day of Christ.

-Philippians 1:10, KJV

Now I beseech you, brethren, mark them which cause divisions and offenses contrary to the doctrine, which you have learned; and avoid them.

-Romans 16:17, KJV

We should understand that we are to be excellent in all things, be sincere in all things, and be without offense in all things. Paul says to the Church at Rome, and by revelation, the church of today, that we need to identify people who bring about divisions and offenses that are contrary to what has been taught. There are a lot of people who are suffering in conditions because they are still holding on to offenses. The consequences of offense are destructive, demolishing, and deadly. That's why we cannot tolerate the ***spirit of offense***. We cannot handle it lightly, and we cannot handle it with a laid-back, casual attitude, because the consequences are too costly and the penalty is too great. There are offenses resting in married couples, parents, children, leaders, people in the body of Christ, employees, employers, politics, and the list goes on. Many are strapping explosives to their souls. All it takes is the wrong person or the wrong situation to push the button, and it will cause an explosion. Many get to that point where life gets out of control, and all of a sudden, they become destructive and deadly.

Every action has a reaction. Everything you do is going to cause something to react in you, against you, or around you. That's why we should be aware of the consequences of not dealing with, not confronting, and not exposing things that happened to us or against us. Offense sets in us if we do not deal with it. There are too many people in the body of Christ who are getting sick or are struggling as they get older. Sometimes, they are being challenged with certain things in their emotions and in their minds. More things seem to fall apart and fall into disarray in their lives. It should be that the longer you serve God, the more blessed your life ought to be. The longer you serve Him, the sweeter He ought to be to you. Still, when we live in this vacillating, mental boxing match of offense, we get to a point where we don't know what to do.

An unresolved issue creates an unresolved crisis.

The ***spirit of offense demonstrated by Cain*** exists when you allow offenses to get in you that are not resolved, corrected, or confronted. This spirit shows us how it spills over and causes your life to literally become hijacked by an attack of the enemy, and causes you to become self-destructive. When you allow unresolved offenses to get inside you and you don't say anything, you don't do anything, or you don't ask God to deliver you, ultimately, you will destroy yourself.

If you let offenses harbor inside of you, the word of God teaches us that **anger, aka 'offense', rests in the bosom of a fool.** The word of God does not say you cannot be angry, but when you let anger rest in you, when you let it tabernacle in you. When you let it inhabit your bosom, you subject yourself to becoming a fool. The Word teaches us that we may be angry, but not to the degree of sinning. Don't live in such a way that you are comfortable with a lifestyle of the sun going down on your wrath. The Bible gives us clear instructions: **God does not want us to**

live with offenses in our lives. It does not matter where it came from or how it happened. The thing that matters is how you are going to conquer the offense that's coming against your life.

So, how are you going to walk in complete victory in your life? At the end of this book, we are going to denounce the spirit of offense as seen in Cain, because there are too many walking around victimized and controlled by the spirit of offense. The type of spirit that attached to Cain is literally manifesting itself in many of our lives and using us to wreak havoc in other people's lives. It's such a subtle spirit because it hides itself in the garments of our personalities. It masquerades as religion, when really it is the result of an offense that has not been confronted or corrected.

***

And Adam knew Eve his wife; and she conceived and bare Cain and said, "I have gotten a man from the Lord." And she again bare his brother Abel and Abel was a keeper of sheep, but Cain was a tiller of the ground.

-Genesis 4:1-2, KJV

Cain was the older brother. He was supposed to be the one who was old enough to take care of his younger brother and mature enough to handle any possible issues. What I am trying to get us to understand is that the older we are in God, the more we are supposed to care for younger Christians and manage possible offenses. The Apostle Paul teaches in the word of God that we are at a place in our lives where we are still drinking milk when we should be eating meat. He says we are supposed to be teaching others to be mature, yet we ourselves still need to be taught how to be mature. That's why he teaches us not to rebuke an elder or an older person, because they are supposed to be mature.

The Word teaches that God also calls the young because they are strong, but the old because they know the way. He is not just speaking about knowing the way of salvation; he is speaking about this: when we have a healthy relationship with God long enough, we are supposed to be mature enough to know how to handle offenses. We are supposed to protect our brothers and sisters. When offenses happen, we are not supposed to be the gas that adds to the fire. We are our brothers' keepers. We are supposed to be the ones who look after them and the ones who correct them when they are wrong. Those of us who have been around the kingdom of God for years are not supposed to be so touchy and sensitive. There are certain things we are supposed to be dead to by now. Our feelings are not supposed to be easily wounded.

I learned recently that when a horse is trained for battle, the trainer shoots a gun near the horse's ear. The first few times, the horse gets frightened by the gunshot because it is something it isn't used to. However, the trainer keeps shooting the gun near the horse's ear so that it does not move when it hears gunshots. The last thing a rider wants to do is ride a horse into battle that's afraid of gunfire. I want to suggest that there are too many of us who have been around wars long enough and are still gunshot fearful, wanting to run, resign, quit, give up, and still getting offended. Perhaps God is saying to you that you have to train yourself for the battle before you get into real warfare, and you've been trained to handle life and life issues. Why are you jumping in response to every noise? What's wrong with you? You are not a cadet; you are a warrior! You didn't just get here; you've been here! It may be challenging, but this is not your first rodeo. You are not some instant cake out of the box; you are a time-tried professional cake, cooked from scratch. You know how to make it, whether whole or on broken pieces. You are not an overnight blunder but a life survivor wonder!

We are supposed to be mature enough now that we can rejoice when falsely persecuted. We need mature people in the kingdom of God. We need people who will show how to keep it together when others fall apart. That's what this young generation is looking for. That's what those who are coming into the church are looking for and need to see. They are not looking for people who are dealing with offenses and are struggling and responding the same way they are. They are looking for people who are dealing with life issues and offenses on earth, but still live like those who are on their way to heaven. We have been trained to win and expect to win! What are we jumping for? We must prophesy to ourselves and say, "I can handle this!"

***

The next thing I want us to see in the life of Cain is how offenses start when we find ourselves insecure in our own assignments, and we start looking down on others' assignments. Competition and jealousy are killers! We are going to renounce the type of spirit that overcame Cain because competition has set up in some of us. It's not that we want what other people have; we just don't want them to have it, and this was Cain's issue. He was a tiller of the ground. That was his life path. Abel was a keeper of the sheep, and that was his life path. Still, somehow, Cain allowed himself to become offended at their different life paths. Cain was looking at his younger brother keeping the sheep while he was tilling the dirt. We must understand that both were going to produce a harvest. If we are always looking at what other people are producing and feeling that they are going to get the upper hand, or that they will have more than we have, we will get offended.

This is the reason so many get offended, and why we find this great battle between many pulpits and pews, because many in the pews somehow feel those in the pulpit will get more than them. Those who allow themselves to feel less than will become critical of those whom they feel are more than. We allow ourselves to become offended over what other people are being or doing instead of appreciating what God has given us to be or called us to do. We fail to realize we can't be everyone else or, for that matter, anyone else. We are not going to have what everyone has. Like someone else's visions or dreams. We must till our own ground and be happy with what God has planned for us.

One of my daughters once wrote something that blessed me. She wrote, "Be and do all that you can be and do." Cain should have realized that tilling the ground was how he would grow the fruits and vegetation so that Abel's sheep could eat. Why would he get jealous of his brother for taking care of the sheep when the sheep ate of what came from his ground? Why sit around upset at what other people are doing, not realizing that they cannot do what they are doing if we don't do what we are doing?

Cain could not handle the fact that his brother (at least to him) seemed to have a more important assignment. There is a social war between those who feel that they are not important and those who feel that they are more important. In some countries, one of the things that contributes to the overthrow of the governments is when those who do not have the things they desire rise and wage war against those who they feel have more than enough. It is called 'the battle between the haves and the have-nots'.

The same thing could happen in our lives if we live in jealousy and surrender to offenses.

There are some who work blue-collar jobs who are offended with some who have gone to college or work white-collar jobs. It takes all kinds of jobs to make the economy work. There is no need for corporate America to belittle the farmers or for the farmers to be jealous of corporate America; they are a team, economically. This is what we need to understand in the kingdom of God as well. It doesn't matter what you are doing or what others are doing. It doesn't matter about our social status. Think about the human body: the feet are as important as the hands. They are all needed to make the body whole and functional.

And in the process of time it came to pass, that Cain brought of the fruit of the ground an offering unto the Lord. And Abel he also brought of the firstlings of his flock and the fat thereof. And the Lord had respect unto Abel and to his offering. But unto Cain and to his offering he had not respect. And Cain was very wroth, and his countenance fell.

-Genesis 4:3-5,KJV

Let us examine how offenses escalate. With Cain and Abel, the issue was not the quality of their offerings. The issue was the quality of their hearts in the offerings. God did not say that Abel gave more than Cain. What God was looking at was the heart of Cain when it came to his offering versus the heart of Abel in his offering. The heart is always a determining factor in whatever we do. It's not about what people give; it's about what is in their hearts when they give. Cain simply took up anything from the ground and went to God and just gave him an offering. His heart was not connected to it. There was no passion, and there was no affection. Abel decided not to give God just any type of offering. He was determined to find the firstling, the best offering, and give it to God.

Offense always begins setting up in our hearts when we start looking at others doing and giving the best that they have, when we know that we are not doing or giving our best. We tend to become very critical and cynical of those who want to give God the best of themselves. The average person gets more excited when a person testifies to being delivered from drugs or coming out of some horrific lifestyle. Thank God for such testimonies; however, when people come to God early in their lives and live for God and don't know anything about clubs, drinking, and smoking, we are not very excited when they testify, and we treat it as if it's no big deal. It somehow says that if people don't go through the dirt, then their testimonies are not worth anything. Every testimony is a testimony. If God brings someone out of the depths of despair, that's a testimony. When God keeps someone from the depths of despair, that's a testimony as well.

So, why would a person be offended when people talk about how much they love God? Offended persons often believe that no one can love God like that. They believe these people are just faking it, but no one can judge how much a person loves God. We don't know how good God has been to those who love him passionately. We must not judge others' worship if we don't love Him the way they love Him. Offended persons say, 'Those people are always talking about God.'

Well, who else should they talk about?

Offended persons may say, 'Those people are always going to church.'

Where else are they to go?

They are Abel worshippers. They love him with excellent praise. There is nothing cheap about their worship. An Abel spirit does not want to give God anything cheap. We must give Him an expensive prayer—time that costs us something, and time that means something to us. We must give him something that costs us something.

Cain-believers in the church will always be offended by Abel-believers because Abel-believers want to give God excellent praise. They are committed to fasting, prayer, being in the face of God, and giving God the best of their service. Cain-believers sit around and get offended. We don't have to be offended when we can be Abel-believers. Cain had the same opportunity that Abel had. Cain could have looked through his garden and found the best pumpkin, the t tomatoes, or the cucumbers. He could have given God the best of whatever he had and taken his time. He could have turned down the average fruits and vegetables because they were not worthy of God and picked the best ones, but he didn't. Abel looked at his sheep and saw a spot on one and perhaps said, "Not you." Maybe he saw one walking with a limp, and he said, "Not you." Most likely, he saw a perfect lamb and said, "This one is worthy of my God! I am giving Him my best offering."

The next thing that happens in the heart of Cain, and that can happen to any of us that offense goes deeper. In this story, God came on the scene, offered Cain an out, but Cain's response was out of offense. When the spirit of offense gets in us, and God tries to speak to us, we find a way of passing the buck or justifying our actions.

And the Lord said unto Cain, why are thy wroth? and why is thy countenance fallen? If thou doest well, shall not thou be accepted?

-Genesis 4:6-8, KJV

All we need to do to be right is to do the right thing.

Now, the issue was not between Cain and Abel because Abel didn't have a problem with Cain; the issue was between God and Cain. If Cain felt he should have been offended, it should have been with God. We cannot be offended when God decides to bless someone. We can't be offended when God raises up other people and moves awesomely in their lives. We see it happen sometimes in the body of Christ, in sports, in business, and other sectors of society. The greatest tragedy is that we see it too often in churches and ministries, especially among pastors, when they see God blessing one ministry and beginning to raise up that ministry. They allow the spirit of offense to rise, and they start talking badly about that ministry because they feel the ministry is not worthy of it. Still, who are we to decide who God should raise up or who God should bless?

Remember, many of the blessings in our lives have nothing to do with whether we are qualified for or worthy of them. They have nothing to do with whether we are good enough for them, if we have the right last name, or live on the right side of town. They have everything to do with the fact that God just looked on us and decided to bless our lives. Why do we get upset when it seems as though others' prayers are being answered, and we are still praying?

God did it, not them!

Why do we get upset because some people's businesses are doing well, and ours are still struggling?

God did it, not them!

Why do we get upset when others get promotions or open doors, move to better houses, or start driving better cars, and we are still believing in God and trusting God? If we learn how to celebrate with others what God is blessing, we will find out that we are getting ready to move into our season, just like them. We are too blessed to be offended. Make this decree:

I don't care who is driving what. I don't care who testifies how the Lord gave them this or that. I don't care who the next one to get married is. I recognize I am blessed of the Lord. I am waiting on God. I am not intimidated. I am not insecure. I don't have low self-esteem. I know who I am, and I am waiting for my season. I will not be offended with others while I am in my waiting season.

The spirit of offense can hold up our prosperity, promises, and power. When the spirit of offense is ruling us, the Amplified Bible says that 'sin crouches at the door.' If we don't get rid of the spirit of offense, it's going to make us kill, sin, and it's going to master us. If we don't deal with this, it is going to lead us into violations of the word of God. The ultimate goal of offense is to master us.

We must not think offense is something to play with. Offended persons will say they just don't want to talk about it. They may say I am processing, and they may ignore the situation by claiming they are protecting their peace. The word of God says sin crouches at our doors because sin is right there waiting for a chance to pounce on us. God says all we must do to shut this door is to do well. If we **don't master this, it will master us.** Cain did not heed the voice of the Lord, and because of it, he killed his brother.

> ***And Cain talked with Abel his brother; and it came to pass, when they were in the field, that Cain rose up against Abel his brother, and slew him.***
>
> ***-Genesis 4:8, KJV***

Offense will lead you to set people up. That's why you must use sharp discernment. **Don't follow offended people.** They will lead you out to the field or purpose for your life, and they will kill you in the field of their own frustration and offense. **Cain asked Abel to go with him into his field and killed Abel there.**

It takes a fool to follow a fool.

The Five Consequences of the Spirit that seized Cain

1. **You shed innocent blood -** Offense will cause you to shed innocent blood **(Gen 4:11)**. People who do you no wrong will become your enemies. People who were not there when you were hurt are now bearing the brunt of your hurts. For example, you didn't know your spouse when you were offended in

some other relationships, but now your spouse is the one who must shed blood because of your offense. You didn't have any children when you went through that offense as a child, but now that you are grown and have children, your children shed their innocent blood because of your offense from childhood.

2. **Your past will never be silent –** Things from your past relationships, deeds, or decisions will still speak to your life, even when you think that you have buried them and moved on with your life **(Gen 4:10).** You will not be able to escape because offense has imprisoned you. You could end up being the kind of person who can't keep a job, position, or anything relational. You find that you are always in some type of relationship conflict because of the screams of offenses.
3. **You become unproductive and unfruitful -** When you till the ground, it shall not henceforth yield unto thee her strength **(Gen 4:12)**. You start out doing something, and it doesn't make you happy. You have numerous opportunities, and none of them make you happy; none of them get completed. Something

must be wrong. According to Psalm 1, I am supposed to prosper in whatsoever I do, but you are never going to prosper if you are always anti-prosperous against other people. You will obtain something good in your life, and for some reason, it won't work out.

4. **You become unstable-** We become vagabonds and fugitives **(Gen 4:13)**. We are on the run all our lives, and it's the spirit of Cain. There are some people who, when they get offended, go from church to church. They do not stay still long enough to become mature and deliver. They always feel led to leave one ministry after the next, and they become unstable. When Jacob was getting ready to bless his son at his death, his oldest son—who was his strength—was so violent and carried on so badly that Jacob told him he was as unstable as water. His son missed out on the inheritance because he was unstable. If we have the spirit of Cain, we are unstable. People don't know how to take us. They don't know if they can trust us. We will be the kind of people who are on today and off tomorrow, in today and out tomorrow, with us today and against

us tomorrow.

5. **You have self-pity-** "And Cain said unto the Lord, my punishment is greater than I can bear." **(Gen 4:13)**. He wasn't saying all of this when he was killing his brother. But now, all of a sudden, he couldn't bear this. When we find ourselves with the spirit of Cain, all we do is focus on ourselves. Self-pitying people usually say, "I have been wronged, I have been hurt." It's I . . . I . . . I, and they never step back and think, *Wait a minute. What did I do to contribute to this? What do I need to do to learn from this? How can I be better because of this? How can I take my pain and produce a better me? How can I take my mess and make it a message?*

We must renounce the spirit of Cain!

The Offense Tool Sheet

Date: ____________________

Time: ____________________

***

What did I learn about myself today?

____

____

____

____

____

What did the Holy Spirit say to me today?

____

____

____

____

____

What victory did I gain today?

____

____

____

____

____

What is my goal for being a better me?

____

____

____

____

____

How will I handle not being offended in the future?

How will I handle not offending others?

What are my plans to not participate in others' offense?

Who am I praying for that's offended?

CHAPTER FOUR

THE SPIRIT OF OFFENSE: *THE COVERT ON SAUL*

The spirit of offense hates the message of this book because it is designed to expose and expel the ***spirit of offense***. It is using every tentacle it has to keep its head protected. It does not care about us cutting off one or all of its tentacles as long as we don't wound the head. Jesus said something along the same lines. He said that if we smite the shepherd, the sheep will scatter. He was communicating that if we destroy the head, the rest of the body will become powerless. We are after the spirit of offense.

> ***That you may approve things that are excellent, that ye may be sincere and without offense till the day of Christ.***
>
> ***-Philippians 1:10, KJV***

The name **"Christ"** literally means **anointing**. What we need to understand about this is that God expects us to be sincere, to walk in excellence, and to have no offense till the anointing shows up. If you can hold on and be sincere and without offense, the anointing will remove the yoke and destroy the burden, through whatever happens in your life. The anointing is not going to show up where there is offense and insincerity. The Word of God, deep in our spirits, is our weapon against the ***spirit of offense***. Every time the enemy tries to come near you or attack you with offense, you must know how to defeat him. It's not just about you being offended; this is also about you not offending people.

The Word of God teaches us that we shouldn't offend the least person. Jesus said if you offend the least one**, it was better for you that a millstone was tied around your neck and be cast into the midst of the sea (Matt 18:6).** We need to understand the seriousness of offense. It is out of control in our personal lives and certainly in the body of Christ and other sectors of society. Some people live life seemingly in an ordinary existence, or serve in some type of leadership capacity, but as soon as you touch the offended part of their mind or life, they self-destruct.

***

Life Is Too Short to Die Without Living

It seems as though the older some people get, the more difficult they become to get along with. The older some get, the more sensitive they become about minor issues or conflicts. Instead of growing in their sensitivity to God, they live still attached to unhealthy cords of their past. There are too many with chips on their shoulders and issues in their hearts. People don't spend much time navigating their lives in order not to upset others' overly sensitive lives. If you are committed to living an offense-sensitive life, you'd better be prepared for a life of constant chaos and confrontations. Remember, people around us don't tolerate our foolishness the way they used to. Even on jobs, people who have ordinarily put up with all kinds of stuff with us at work now tell us to leave, and employers will fire us right away.

The ***spirit of offense in Saul*** is the most dangerous manifestation of the spirit of offense. When the Spirit of the Lord ministered this word and the revelation of it to my spirit, it changed my life. I pray that if you have any sense of God about you, it will make you guard your heart like never before. The Word of God teaches us that God told

Samuel to anoint Saul as king. Saul did not go looking for the job of king. He was looking for his father's donkeys. God selected Saul and told the man of God to anoint him. So, first, he was anointed.

The second thing we know about him is that he was a handsome man. He was head and shoulders above everybody. The Word says he was a good-looking, tall man, and God anointed him. He should not have been insecure, but even in his anointing, there existed a flaw in his spirit. Often, we are so moved by people's anointing that we overlook the flaws in their spirits. Many offended people are anointed. They can preach, and they can sing, but we don't know what's going on in their spirits. We must be very discerning, so that we aren't moved by people's gifts. Some preachers will preach tremendous words, walk out of the pulpit, and commit moral failures, but we must not be deceived or discouraged.

***

Gifted Does Not Mean Godly

In 1 Samuel 13, Saul was anointed, but he spent the remainder of his life as a king looking for people to affirm him. They didn't anoint him; God did, but he looked more to people than he did to God.

And he tarried seven days, according to the set time of Samuel had appointed; but Samuel came not to Gilgal and the people were scattered from him.

-1 Samuel 13:8, KJV

Let's examine how the spirit of offense worked against Saul and how it can start working against us. It can start when we spend all our lives constantly needing people to affirm us. We must not set ourselves up for people to let us down. It is the nature of people to let us down. I don't care how wonderful they are or how sincere they mean to be to us; people will let us down. We must not spend all our lives constantly counting on and depending on people to affirm and build us up. Somewhere along the line, we will be disappointed. If we don't handle our disappointment right, we are setting ourselves up for offense.

Therefore said I, the Philistines would come down now upon me to Gilgal, and I have not made supplication unto the Lord; I forced myself therefore, and offered a burnt offering.

-I Samuel 13:12, KJV

We see Saul start down the road of offense. I want to show you some things that we must watch for to make sure that we're guarded against the spirit of Saul.

And Saul also went home to Gibeah; and there went with him a band of men whose hearts God had touched.

-1 Samuel 10:26-27, KJV

Many times, our greatest tests of offense are going to be at home. Sometimes, people say to me, "I can really flow when I am ministering away from my home church. I can really sing, get in the anointing when I am away from home." Still, the greatest test of the authenticity of our anointing is always going to be in environments where we are familiar. Jesus went through the same thing, and I don't know why we think we are so different.

The Word of God says Jesus went to his own hometown and could only do a few miracles because of unbelief. The Word gives an account of the people's reaction to Jesus: They said of him that he is the son of Mary and Joseph, and his sisters live right here with us. He went away from home. Now, he is back, proclaiming to be the Messiah. We know who he is (Mark 6:3, KJV). One of the most challenging things about growing up and doing what God has called us to do is the failure of people to see our transitions. Focusing on their failure can lead to self-inflicted offenses. If you are a victim of this type of offense, make a decision today to change your life for yourself. You don't have to force yourself on others. That can be as offensive to others as they were to you. Let it be that when we return from where were, people will see that we are not what we were but who we are.

You must know that the power of your transition is not proven in the face of people who don't know you. The power of your transition is always proven in the face of people who knew you before you changed. The true test of your transformation will be the acknowledgement by those who knew you before the transformation. Why should they say that? Because they knew you then, and they see you now! That's the power of transformation.

People who don't know you can't prove your transformation.

I want you to understand how we tend to allow ourselves to get offended. In the Word, Saul went home, and there was a group of men whose hearts were touched by God towards Saul. These were valiant men and mighty men who went along with and celebrated Saul.

> ***But the children of Belial said, how shall this man save us?***
>
> ***-1 Samuel 13:27, KJV***

Still, the children of Belial knew Saul before. So, when he returned to his home with these mighty men, the children of Belial (worthless people) asked how this man could save them.

> ***And they despised him, and brought him no presents. But he held his peace.***
>
> ***-1 Samuel 10:27, KJV***

It is dangerous to begin letting things get into your soul, don't say anything, or confront the issues. It is dangerous not to vent, let it out, not deal with it, and just carry it. Saul didn't say anything. Perhaps, all he did was continually repeat what those worthless people were saying about him in his mind or out of his mouth. When people start saying negative things about you, even if you can't say anything to them, start speaking positively to yourself. You get in front of a mirror, and you prophesy greatness over yourself. I don't care what they say about you; you get in a mirror, and you tell yourself how you have been fearfully and wonderfully made. Say who you are and what you are until you see who you are and what you are.

And Eliab his eldest brother heard what he spake unto the men; and Eliab's anger was kindled against David, and he said, Why camest thou down hither? And with whom hast thou left those few sheep in the wilderness? I know thy pride, and the naughtiness of thine heart; for thou art come down that thou mightest see the battle.

-1 Samuel 17:28, KJV

One of the results of the spirit of offense that attacked Saul was his being despised by his own brothers. Offenses do not typically happen with people we are not in relationship with. David's oldest brother despised him.

Why did Eliab despise David?

Because God anointed him in Eliab's father's house. There are times when we can allow offenses to come into our lives when we feel we didn't get what others received. Perhaps Eliab felt that he was the oldest and should have been the one anointed. Many times, people look at the outward appearance, but God looks at the heart. We must not get offended over the people whom God has anointed. We can't go through life upset because certain ones have certain gifts and graces on their lives. God anointed David, so why would Eliab get offended? He despised David and said that David was full of pride. It's amazing how we call people what we are ourselves.

> ***And David said, what have I now done? Is there not a cause?***
>
> ***-I Samuel 17:29, KJV***

Obviously, something existed between these two brothers before this incident because David asked, "Now, what have I done?" Have you ever gone to people who are offended with you and asked them, 'What have I done, now?' This thing that happened between the two of them was most critical when Israel was in its most crucial time, facing its greatest enemy. David inquired as to why they were afraid of this giant, who was defiling all the nations of Israel and the God of Israel. David stood up and said it didn't have to be like that. His brother's response, out of his offense, was that David came to the battle out of pride.

His brother despised him.

We must not despise others, because we are in the same family of God. When the Lord uses certain people, we should not despise them. We must stop this in the body of Christ. When others build nice buildings and churches, we respond, "Well, you know, I just wouldn't have built anything that big. I just wouldn't have gotten into such debt," but that's not our assignment. There is no reason for that when we are all in the body of Christ.

The second thing we see happen is in 1 Samuel 17:31-33. Saul sent for David, and we can find ourselves escalating into the grips of the spirit of Saul. We find ourselves sending for or calling for people to come into our lives who don't ask to be in there. Why do we invite people into our lives to get offended with them? Why do we marry people and not treat them right? Why do we have children and abuse them? We are the ones who invite these people into our lives. How can people adopt children and then abuse them? If we are not going to treat people right, we must leave their lives alone. If we are not going to love our children, we should give them up for adoption. We must not invite people into our lives and abuse them. These are souls, and **we are supposed to be a benefit and a blessing to people.** When they come into your life, their lives are supposed to be better because of you.

In the midst of this, Saul gives David all his weapons to put on. First of all, he is despised; secondly, he is sent for, and thirdly, he is attempted to be made over. When you find yourself starting down this road, you will always try to change people into who you think they ought to be. You will get your feelings hurt because people are not going to let you change them. Unfortunately, some have been to Saul's extreme makeover camp. Still, the truth is that **we can't change people who don't want to change.** That's between God and them. We can't marry someone and say, "I want you to be like someone else." We spend all this energy trying to change people because we are offended, and we think that it's our responsibility to change them, but we can't change people. We can't make people love us who have decided to hate us. We can give people the shirts off our backs, and they will laugh at our nakedness.

Saul essentially said, 'Here, take this; put this on.' The Spirit of the Lord showed me that David's refusal of Saul's garments was the last thing that really pushed Saul over the edge. If David had gone out and fought Goliath with Saul's garments on and won, Saul could have rightfully claimed some of the victory. If David had gone to battle with Saul's weapons on and killed Goliath, then Saul could have said, 'It was because of my weapons that David won. That was my stuff. See! That was my weapon; that was my shield.' But when David turned down his stuff, Saul had no claim to David's victory.

Sometimes, when we refuse to allow people to change us, and we remain anointed regardless of their efforts, they can't handle it. They don't have the right to say, 'I helped them become what they are.' **My liberation day came when I decided once and for all to be only what God wants me to be!** If others liked it, we could get along. If others didn't like it, we could get along. When we have embraced the spirit of Saul, one of the questions we need to answer is why we are always trying to change people. We are taking on each other's stuff but losing our own identities. When we do that, eventually, we wake up and realize we've lost ourselves. We don't know who we are, and that's when we start allowing people to tell us, every day, who we are supposed to be. The most miserable people in the world are those who are lost and don't know how to get back to where they need to be. We must know who we are.

***

The Consequences of the Spirit of Saul

> ***And Saul was very wroth, and the saying displeased him; and he said, They have ascribed unto David ten thousand, and to me they ascribed but thousands: and what can have more but the kingdom?***
>
> ***-I Samuel 18:8-11, KJV***

One consequence of this type of spirit is unprovoked anger. When we find ourselves having problems with other people being complimented, we are on very dangerous ground. When we find ourselves constantly struggling with or feeling uneasy and uncomfortable with others' success, that is not a good sign. When somebody says, "That's a wonderful singer," and you reply, "But I heard a few off notes," then we find ourselves having problems with others complimenting other people, and that's not healthy. When we find ourselves in positions in which nobody is complimenting us, we need to compliment ourselves. That's not arrogance. Arrogance is when we feel we are better than anyone else. Confidence teaches us that we are just as good as anyone else.

After David killed Goliath, the women sang, "Saul killed thousands, but David killed his ten thousand." They just went on and on, and suddenly, that green-eyed monster rose up in Saul. The person that he sent for was the person who had gotten him out of hot water. According to the war protocol, had the Philistines won the challenge, Saul would have been the first killed; so, David really delivered Saul. Now, Saul had a problem with the women complimenting David. We must learn how to appreciate other people and appreciate them being admired.

And it came to pass on the morrow, that the evil spirit from God came upon Saul, and he prophesied in the midst of the house: and David played with his hand, as at other times: and there was a javelin in Saul's hand.

-1 Samuel 18:10, KJV

Do you see the tragic state of an offended person? They have offended spirits and still want to prophesy. They have offended spirits and are yet ministering. They are angry yet are leading worship. They are mean as junkyard dogs, yet they want to usher others into the presence of God. The Bible says Saul had already become angry over what they were singing about David. He then went into the house of God with religion and offense. He couldn't help himself because he was controlled by the ***spirit of offense***. The Bible says Saul took a javelin and threw it at David in an attempt to kill him, and the spirit of offense always produces unprovoked anger.

We must guard our hearts so that we don't minister to God's people, or whatever else we are doing in life, with polluted hands. We don't consider that what we are doing is going to have ramifications in our lives. This is when we have utterance and function with no power.

The following are verses of scripture that will get us through any attack of offense and will bless our lives.

And David behaved himself wisely in all his ways; and the Lord was with him.

-1 Samuel 18: 14, KJV

David's attitude to Saul was, I am not coming down to your level. That should be our reaction to offended people.

You can be offended, but I am not coming down on your level.

> ***Wherefore, when Saul saw that he behaved himself very wisely he was afraid of him. But all Israel and Judah loved David, because he went out and came in before them.***
>
> ***-1 Samuel 18:15-16, NRSV***

The people kept looking at David to see how he was going to respond to Saul's attack. They may not ever tell us, but there are always people watching us to see how we respond to offense. When they see how we handle it, they will love us more.

First Samuel 18-31 is filled with the attacks of Saul against David. Saul's only motivation was to destroy David. When we are offended and get the spirit of Saul in us, our only satisfaction is going to be the day we destroy the person we are offended by. We will hunt them down and make up stuff if we have to. We will do whatever it takes to achieve our goal. So, Saul threw another javelin at David in 1 Samuel 19:9-10. He was enraged with David, and David had done nothing to Saul but deliver him from the

Philistines, and Saul repaid David by throwing another javelin at him. Saul then sent messengers to watch David with the intent of killing him (v. 11-15).

When we get the spirit of offense as Saul did in our lives, we seek to form offense allies. We align with people who enable us, whether we are in person or absent from the moment. We may not be there, but we have messengers there for us. They give a report to us of everything that goes on or is said. One thing worse than having a spirit of offense like Saul is the people who serve those with the spirit of offense like Saul. They do the dirty work for the Sauls.

Consider what these messengers did as they went to David's house. As a result, Saul turned against his own daughter because she helped her husband escape. Those with a spirit of offense will attempt to cause others to turn against us because we won't destroy others for their benefit. They work to cause us to treat others the way they think we ought to treat them. We often cater to them out of a sense of obligation or false loyalty. If we are not careful, those with a spirit of offense will turn on us and will threaten us if we don't do what they want us to do. If we do, then they promise to accept us.

Then Saul turned against Jonathan, his own son, in 1 Samuel 20:30. He called Jonathan perverted and rebellious. Why? Because Jonathan did not go along with his offended spirit. I respect people who don't feed others' offenses, even if they are family members. We must not ever allow ourselves to condone people when they are wrong. If they're wrong, they're wrong. Jonathan realized that there was something special about David, so he chose not to go along with his father to destroy David. Saul was so offended that he turned against his own son, proving that the spirit of offense cares about no one. It only cares about what it wants, and whoever gets in its way experiences its wrath.

According to 1 Samuel 22:16-19, Saul sent killers to David's house and his own daughter's house. He threw another javelin at the focus of his offense. Saul became so enraged that he killed all 45 priests who he felt protected David. He then burned down the entire city and killed all of their animals. When offense gets in us, and we don't confront and conquer it, an out-of-control rage is the result.

Consider what happens in 1 Samuel 23:7. It is quite sad. Saul thought God was with him and delivered David into his hand because when he went into the city, Saul had killed the priests and destroyed the city, and he was convinced that God was with him. Saul was convinced God delivered David into his hands, and when the spirit of offense operates in us, we can be absolutely wrong and be convinced we are absolutely right. We don't want to be like that. We don't want to think that we are on the right track and are wrong the entire time. There ought to be something about the God in us that makes us want to be righteous and right.

Let's look at 1 Samuel 23:25-28, 24:2-17, and 26:7-25. These are the most powerful confrontations in the whole story of David and Saul. It is in chapter 24 that David cut Saul's robe. David had a chance to kill Saul right then, but he did not do it. Then Saul repented and said to David, "You are a better man than I am," but as soon as the offended spirit rose up again, he was right back attempting to kill David. Just because we don't feel angry now does not mean that we are delivered. We have to go after this monster constantly to kill it.

The conclusion of the spirit of Saul can be found in 1 Samuel 28:7-12. Saul went to the witch at Endor and ended up in witchcraft because of the spirit of offense. In the last scripture in 1 Samuel 31:4-9, he died in a battle. His head was cut off and paraded through the country of the Philistines. The same people who David delivered Saul from when he killed Goliath were the ones who killed him. What made Saul's life end so tragically? It was an uncontrolled spirit of offense that caused him to die. If we are carrying the spirit of offense, we must repent. If we are unable to break free of this spirit, we need to be delivered.

The Offense Tool Sheet

Date: ____________________

Time: ____________________

***

What did I learn about myself today?

____

____

____

____

____

What did the Holy Spirit say to me today?

____

____

____

____

____

What victory did I gain today?

____

____

____

____

____

What is my goal to be a better me?

____

____

____

How will I handle not being offended in the future?

How will I handle not offending others?

What are my plans to not participate in others' offense?

Who am I praying for that's offended?

CHAPTER FIVE

THE SPIRIT OF OFFENSE: *THE SNIPER*

One of the most needed shifts in this season for the body of Christ and the world is the shift from:

- Immaturity: the inability or unwillingness to function or act fully developed. The issue of immaturity is holding many back on many levels from reaching their maximum potential.

- Selfishness: a continual culture of desires and decisions driven by self-gratification.

- Self-centeredness: the 'me' attitude above any effect or impact on corporate betterment.

One of the hindrances to this shift will be an overwhelming presence and submission to the spirit of offense. This spirit is most dangerous because of the ability and skill as a sniper.

And then shall many be offended, and shall betray one another, and shall hate one another.

-Matthew 24:10, KJV

Offense tends to operate through the means of the sniper:

- Sniper: to shoot at exposed individuals from an unusual, concealed point of vantage.

- Sniperscope: an optical device for use especially with a rifle that allows a person to see targets better in the dark.

Woe unto the world because of offences! for it must needs be that offences come; but woe to that man by whom the offence cometh!

-Matthew 18:7, KJV

If the spirit of the ruler rise up against thee, leave not thy place; for yielding pacifieth great offences.

-Ecclesiastes 10:4 KJV

King David's, of the scriptures, greatest attacks came from people who were offended, but he did not retaliate:

- Saul was offended to jealousy.
- Amnon was offended to lust.
- Absalom was offended to rebellion.
- Ahithophel was offended to betrayal.
- The Gibeonites were offended to revenge.

As you read this chapter, try doing a self-analysis. It is easy to look through a window and see others, but true growth occurs when you can look in a mirror and see yourself.

Do you find yourself dealing with and thus living with some of these tendencies consistently? You may be offended or an offender.

- Suspicious of innocent people without cause.
- Needy of unhealthy attention, directly or indirectly.
- Instigators of constant confusion with little or no desire for peace.
- Prideful of your ability and the belittling of others
- Emotional at every situation without a resolution as the objective.

- Rebellious to authority with no cause and no remorse for actions.

Offense will destroy marriages, families, friendships, health, finances, ministries, businesses, nations. The sniper shoots and kills indiscriminately.

Here's how the sniper of the offense spirit works to achieve its highest goal of destruction:

- It apprehends and assassinates your heart.

A brother offended is harder to be won than a strong city: and their contentions are like the bars of a castle.

-Proverbs 18:19, KJV

- It aggravates and assaults your peace

And when he was come into his own country, he taught them in their synagogue, insomuch that they were astonished, and said, Whence hath this man this wisdom, and these mighty works? Is not this the carpenter's son? Is not his mother called Mary? And his brethren, James, and Joses, and Simon, and Judas? And his sisters, are they not all with us? Whence then hath this man all these things? And they were offended in him. But Jesus said unto them, A prophet is not without honour, save in his own country, and in his own house. And he did not many mighty works there because of their unbelief.

- Matthew 13:54-58, KJV

How many people in the city needed a miracle but did not receive one because of the existence of the spirit of offense? Has offense stopped you from receiving?

- It causes the abandoning of your assignments.

Now when John had heard in the prison the works of Christ, he sent two of his disciples, and said unto him, <u>Art thou he that should come, or do we look for another?</u> Jesus answered and said unto them, Go and shew John again those things which ye do hear and see: The blind receive their sight, and the lame walk, the lepers are cleansed, and the deaf hear, the dead are raised up, and the poor have the gospel preached to them. And blessed is he, whosoever shall not be offended in me.

- Matthew 11:2-6, KJV

- It assassinates your opportunity and derails your destiny.

And, behold, one came and said unto him, Good Master, what good thing shall I do, that I may have eternal life? The young man saith unto him, All these things have I kept from my youth up: what lack I yet? Jesus said unto him, If thou wilt be perfect, go and sell that thou hast, and give to the poor, and thou shalt have treasure in heaven: and come and follow me. But when the young man heard that saying, he went away sorrowful: for he had great possessions.

- Matthew 19:16, 20-22, KJV

- It seeks to destroy your life and looks for you to assist in the suicide.

Then Jezebel sent a messenger unto Elijah, saying, so let the gods do to me, and more also, if I make not thy life as the life of one of them by tomorrow about this time. And when he saw that, he arose, and went for his life, and came to Beer–sheba, which belongeth to Judah, and left his servant there. But he himself went a day's journey into the wilderness, and came and sat down under a juniper tree: and he requested for himself that he might die; and said, It is enough; now, O Lord, take away my life; for I am not better than my fathers.

-1 Kings 19:2-4, KJV

Look at the environment in which the sniper attacked Elijah: in Beersheba and Judah.

- Beersheba, spiritually, represents a place of covenants, divine reassurance, and spiritual boundaries.
- Judah spiritually represents a place of praise and thanksgiving.

How does a person live and be sniper-proof?

Rule your spirit, soul, mind, and body by living submitted and sensitive to the Holy Spirit and the Word of God!

> ***The discretion of a man deferreth his anger; and it is his glory to pass over a transgression.***
>
> ***- Proverbs 19:11, KJV***

> ***He that is slow to anger is better than the mighty; and he that ruleth his spirit than he that taketh a city.***
>
> ***- Proverbs 16:32, KJV***

The Offense Tool Sheet

Date: ____________________

Time: ____________________

***

What did I learn about myself today?

____
____
____
____
____

What did the Holy Spirit say to me today?

____
____
____
____
____

What victory did I gain today?

____
____
____
____
____

What is my goal to be a better me?

____
____
____

How will I handle not being offended in the future?

How will I handle not offending others?

What are my plans to not participate in others' offense?

Who am I praying for that's offended?

CHAPTER SIX

SAFEGUARDS AGAINST OFFENSES: *PROTECTING THE HEART*

Offense knows no limitations. The revelation of the spirit of offense is one of the most liberating teachings that the Spirit of God has given me. It is not something to be taken lightly by anyone, regardless of our status in life. It acts as a terminal illness and is a slow killer. It cannot be downplayed or overlooked. We can't even play with it by jokingly accusing people of having a spirit of offense. The results of these offenses are too serious to joke about. Some of us are genuinely offending people by saying they are offended.

So, how do we safeguard our spirits against the spirit of offense? How do we ensure that it does not set up in us and literally choke us to death spiritually, emotionally, or even worse, physically?

I will go and return to my place, till they acknowledge their offense and seek my face; in their affliction, they will seek me early.

-Hosea 5:15, KJV

Let us look at five particulars about the spirit of offense and see their impact. I then want to provide seven ways to safeguard our spirits, our families, our ministries, and our relationships against the spirit of offense.

That you may approve things that are excellent, that ye may be sincere and without offense till the day of Christ.

-Philippians 1:10, KJV

This Scripture is our ultimate goal, and it is the high mark we want to reach. It is where we should be striving to live, and the will of God that we excel in all things. When my life is not constantly excelling, I need to stop long enough to ask myself what's going on because it is God's will for my life to excel. It is God's will that all of our lives continue to excel.

Still, Paul says not only should we excel, but we should also be sincere. That means I am not to be a fake or a phony. I am not to have a false presentation of myself. God's will is that we be sincere about life, purpose, and, most of all, our walk with Christ. We are in a life-or-death fight. This is so serious, my brothers and sisters, because we will give an account for every word we speak or think. The Apostle Paul says to be sincere in all things. He also says to be without offense in all things. I cannot expect to excel or be sincere if I am living with offense. Paul teaches us to be offense-free until the day of Christ's reappearance. He lets us know that we do not have a right to expect the anointing to show up in our lives when we have offenses or when we are not sincere or when we don't have a desire to excel.

***

Five Components Needed to Guard Against Offense

It is important for those of us who are perpetually cantankerous and adversarial to understand that this should not be our personality or demeanor. If we were like that, once we came to Christ, we should have taken on the nature of Christ. We should have the love and characteristics of the heavenly Father.

A brother offended is harder to be won than a strong city; and there contentions are like the bars of a castle

-Proverbs 18:19, KJV

The First Thing: Don't Be an Offended Brother

Proverbs teaches that once we are offended, it is very difficult for us to be won over. It is easier to go to war and to conquer a strong city than to win over someone who is offended. When we allow the spirit of offense to take root in our lives, people can apologize, they can repent to us, and we will not change.

Why?

It's because we have allowed the spirit of offense to become the controlling agent in our hearts. While some are reading this book, they are seeing some people on the screens of their minds who they have been trying to work with for the longest time, but who haven't changed yet. Sometimes in life, we must know when to leave some people to their own devices. When we have shown people the truth or when we have spoken the word of God to them and they refuse to listen, it's time to say, 'Check you later.' An offended brother is difficult to win, which is what the scripture is telling us. That's why we should not let the spirit of offense build up in our lives. We should not allow the spirit of offense to become so dominant in our lives that we become unreasonable.

Once we become unreasonable, we become unreachable. Once we become unreachable, we become unredeemable. We don't want to be the person other people avoid. There are several people whom I have met over my life that, even when they are shown the word of God in its simplest form, refuse to come under correction. It is very dangerous to get to that place in our lives and in our minds that our feelings and offenses mean more to us than the power and authority of the word of God.

And have no root in themselves, and so endure but for a time; afterward, when affliction or persecution arises for the word's sake; immediately, they are offended.

-Mark 4:17, KJV

The Second Thing: Don't Be Offended by the Word of God

The next thing we must guard ourselves against is being offended by the word of God. Oftentimes, when we hear the word of God, it seems as though our lives come under such attack. We find ourselves offended at the Word. Jesus said the reason that this happens is that we don't have any root in ourselves. We don't have any depth in ourselves. As soon as a little something comes along that touches our little feelings, we get offended.

The thing that the enemy hates more than anything is to be exposed. When we expose the spirit of offense, that's when we can get rid of it. If we are not rooted enough when the word of God comes forth and when trials and tribulations come forth, we are offended for the Word's sake. Jesus said that the word of God is going to offend us. The enemy is coming to try the word of God that we hear.

The Third Thing: Protect the Anointing Against Offense

In 1 Samuel 18:8-12, there is a sad commentary of a man who had everything going for himself, but lost it all because of an offense. It seems as if the most gifted people are the most prone to offend. The people who have more going for them than others can become easily offended if they are not careful.

And Saul was very wroth, and the saying displeased him; and he said, They have ascribed unto David ten thousands and to me they have ascribed but thousands: and what can he have more but the kingdom?

-1 Samuel 18:8, KJV

Saul became offended because he thought David was going to take something from him. Saul was a tall, good-looking, anointed, and rich king. He had all the money, and he could have had all the women. David was not thinking about being a king, but when we get offended, all of a sudden, we get suspicious of everyone. Saul was the anointed man who became offended. We must not be jealous of what someone else has because it destroys what we have. Those of us who have so much going for us have so much purpose. We have so much destiny. Why become envious because someone has one lamb when we have ninety-nine?

Saul's whole life was destroyed because he did not value his purpose or his anointing.

And it came to pass on the morrow that the evil spirit from God came upon Saul and he prophesied in the midst of the house: and David played with his hand as at other times: and there was a javelin in Saul's hand.

-1 Samuel 18:10, KJV

The Bible does not teach us that God sent an evil spirit to Saul, for God does not send evil spirits to people. What the Bible is teaching us is that God undoubtedly had been dealing with Saul about his offense; when he refused to acknowledge it, God stepped back from Saul the same way He did from Cain. He told Cain that if he did not deal with his issue, Satan would be crouching at his door. What God is saying to us is that if we don't deal with our offenses, He is going to step back and let the evil spirit (anger, rebellion, or whatever it may be) come after us. We need to understand that if we don't listen to God, we are going to listen to someone.

Saul had an evil spirit come upon him, and then he tried to prophesy. How many of us have been trying to minister to people who are offended while we ourselves are offended? When offense is transferred to offense, the result is a double case of offense. God will cut us off from our potential and turn us over to our destructive natures and mindsets. Essentially, God said to Saul, 'Don't be like this. Come on, Saul. How can you be mad with the little boy that I sent to deliver you?' But Saul became even more offended with David.

We must not allow our anointing to become offensive or offended. We have become so careless in the house of God, willing to accept anything from anyone as long as they appear to be anointed. Our attitude appears to be, *I don't have to concern myself about how dirty your hands are as long as you entertain me or make me look good or feel good.* We can't do anything big for God by being touchy and feely and not wanting to be corrected. We must be mature in this season in the body of Christ, as we are the new wine generation.

***

The Fourth Thing: Guard Against Offense in Assignment

> ***Giving no offense in anything, that the ministry be not blamed.***
>
> ***-2 Corinthians 6:3, KJV***

We have to make sure the ministry is not offended or offensive. In other words, we must be sure that we carry ourselves in such a way that people don't associate the ministry with our actions. When people get offended at the ministry, they leave the ministry and carry such offenses until they make it their business to go out and tear it down. We are ultimately accountable for what we cause people to think about God's ministry. Paul says the ministry should not be blamed for our offenses. We may do all we can, but some people are still going to be offended because they have that kind of spirit.

It is also the case that sometimes, God will use offense to drive offense out of us. A good way to know if this is happening is to see how often we are offended. If we are always offended over every little thing, it's a good indication that God is using those situations to get us to see what is in us. After all, we have heard that iron sharpens iron.

***

The Fifth Thing: Ensure Others Are Not Offended

Give none offense, neither to the Jews, nor to the Gentiles, nor to the church of God.

-1 Corinthians 10:32, KJV

We must make sure that other Christians are not offended. Paul teaches us that we need to be sure that we are not offending other people in the body of Christ—not just our local ministries, our denominations, our fellowships or associations—but the whole body of Christ. I need to be sure that I'm living and carrying myself and maintaining relationships in such a way that it is not going to be offensive to the body of Christ.

We have talked about these five areas that we want to watch. Now, let us look at some of the safeguards. These safeguards will help all of us; however, God can't help us until we want help. Some people will spend the rest of their lives running, being offended, and shedding innocent blood. They will be cursed in relationships, unproductive, unfruitful, and unstable. They will have self-pity and will not allow the Spirit of God to bring wholeness to their spirits.

The only way offense is going to get out of us is if we allow God to take it out of us. God will take it out of us only when we recognize our need and cry out for His help. I am not giving a quickie solution to what we are dealing with because some of us have been in this so long, it's going to take a literal journey to get free. Still, it's worth it to be free. I have decided for myself to live an offense-free life, and this is the point to which you also must come. I don't care what it is, who it is, or how long it has been, you must decide that you are not going to allow this to control the rest of your life.

***

Building Our Safeguards

Make an Honest Assessment

The first step in building safeguards against offense is doing honest assessments of ourselves. We must stop long enough to say, 'God, this is my problem,' or long enough to ask Him what our problems are.

Why am I like this?

What's going on with me?

We must understand this because it is so important for you and me to begin to see ourselves as God sees us. Until we can do that, we are not going to walk in freedom. We must ask ourselves these kinds of questions:

- Why am I so touchy?
- Why do I find myself getting so angry?
- Why am I so rebellious?
- Why am I so distrustful?
- Why do I constantly find myself in the midst of division and discord?
- Why do I find myself constantly fighting battles of infirmity?
- Why do I find myself continuing to hold on to unforgiveness?
- Why do I constantly complain about how hard it is?

There are things that we need to look at, but we must do diagnostic overviews of ourselves. Until we can do that, we are not going to be free, and we are not going to be delivered. We may have breaks from some storms. We may have little commercials of relief, but we will never be completely free until we make honest assessments of ourselves and put the finger right where the finger belongs.

Fully Work Through Issues

The second step in building safeguards against offense is to work through our issues and not just go through them. This is challenging to us because we are so accustomed to somebody pouring oil on us, laying hands on us, calling stuff out of us, or prophesying to us, and we think that's the end of it. To get over offense, we have to work at it. We have to work on ourselves. We have to sit alone with ourselves. We cannot go to a restaurant with our friends and ask them what they think we should do. **We don't need offense interventions; we need divine intervention.** We are already messed up from constantly listening to other people. Enough!

The worst fear many of us have is the fear of being by ourselves with God and the truth about ourselves. I find myself, as I am riding up and down the road, saying to God, *'How can I be better? Teach me about myself. Show me where I got off track. Show me where I am wrong. Show me whether or not I am offended.'* I must have a clear conscience towards God and towards man.

To those who have gone through horrible situations, I cannot imagine how horrible it was, and yet, you survived it! You did not get a Nobel Prize. What I am telling you is that there will come a time when we must sit alone with ourselves and work through it. We must be willing to cry, adjust, pull off some things, put on some things, and be willing to be honest. We must also be willing to be transparent.

We just can't go through stuff. We just can't come out of one relationship and all of a sudden be in another relationship. We must stop the drama long enough to come off the stage, get a view of the stage, and decide how we are going to change the scenery. This is the hard part because it means working through offense and asking ourselves these questions:

- What did I learn from this?

- Why am I constantly drawing these types of people into my life?
- What did that last experience do to me?
- We must be willing to do this.

We can't just deal with things on the surface, but we must work through these issues. Failure to work through issues can be a major problem for couples. When something happens in their relationship, they just figure time heals all wounds. They don't talk about it or work it through. They deny it long enough until they have forgotten about it, but when it manifests itself again, they still haven't fixed the problem. That's why years later, when something small and insignificant happens, they snap. It wasn't that incident that made them snap; it was years of offenses that they never dealt with, that they didn't work through.

We must work through our offenses. We must take some time to be healed and delivered. If we are going to talk with somebody, we must talk to somebody who is going to tell us the truth about ourselves. We must not go to another wounded or offended person who is going to be on our side when we are just as wrong as the left shoe on the right foot. If we do decide to tell other people our stories, we must tell them the whole story.

Being Prayerful, Patient, and Practical

We are not going to stay offense-free if we don't pray. We must ask the Lord to show us where we are wrong: *God, what could I have done that would have changed the outcome of this situation?* It's going to take some time to get ourselves together, but we must not let it be a long, drawn-out time. We must be patient with ourselves, patient with God, and learn to behave. We have to have the grace on us to deal with offended people and ourselves when we are offended.

Then, we must be practical. By practical, I mean we must do some common-sense stuff. If there are people who we get ticked off by, we must stay away from them until we get some power. We know certain people who push our buttons and stay away from them. This is practical. For example, we can change our seats if they normally sit close to us. We must know what we can handle at that moment. Sometimes, there is nothing wrong with walking away. We must know when we have enough grace to run *from* a race but not to run *in* the race.

Commit Consistently to an Extreme Makeover

We must make ourselves over—not just on the surface, not just that part of us that we want to deal with, but the ugly side of us as well. That may mean changing some relationships. That may mean when we used to be timid and bashful, and people used to push us around and get over on us, we now tell people that we are not timid and bashful. We declare that we have been pushed into our last offense match. We must come to a point where we say, **'Not today!'**

If we are going to do anything for God or have anything in God, we have to be tough enough to be talked about. We must know how to handle offense and offended people if we are going to be anything in God. If we just want to be quiet sitters, the most we can expect is the devil to mess with us. However, if we do anything for God, the devil and some folks in the body of Christ will come after us. If we can't handle that, we are not ready to be blessed and to be a blessing.

Distinguishing the Major Issues from the Minor Incidents

We must learn to identify principles from incidents. Many of us get offended over minor stuff. *Why get worked up over small stuff? Why get offended over stuff that really doesn't mean anything? Why are we carrying stuff against people who have long forgotten about it?* Offended people look for offensive situations. When we are offended, we hear with offensive ears; we see with offensive eyes. Some of us are offended by people because of stuff that their relatives were offended by. We weren't involved in those matters and probably don't have all the facts. *Why are we getting worked up over stuff that's not even our concern?*

This is what happened to Saul. Saul became angry with Jonathan because Jonathan wouldn't back him up in his offense. Saul said Jonathan was perverted and his mother was rebellious. We must know whether something is a minor thing or a major problem. If it's major, only the people who are directly affected should be involved. Offenses spread around the church when we get everybody involved in the matter. If it is major, only the people who are directly affected should be involved. Offenses spread around the church when we get everybody involved in the matter. If it is major, we must keep offense out of it and handle it the biblical way.

A real friend is someone who will not enable you to be offended. We must love people enough that we are willing to risk friendships to tell them what's right.

Offense also feeds on perception. Much of the stuff people do that offends us is nothing more than stuff we perceive. It is not the truth; it's just our reality. What the devil does is put thoughts in our minds and creates an environment to make the thoughts seem real. He puts into our minds that no one likes us and then makes us offended with certain people. As we walk past them, they drop something out of their hands and must reach down to pick it up, thereby avoiding eye contact with us. Then, the devil tells us, *see, they don't want to speak to you. They dropped that on purpose.* How many times have we gone crazy and stayed up all night thinking about stuff, and when we finally talk to the person about it, it was nothing like what we thought? Look at all the energy wasted because we majored in the minor.

Release to Recover, Repent to Restore

If we are going to safeguard ourselves, we must always be willing to release people. The more we hold on to people, the more offended we become. You say you can't just let them go? Okay, hold onto them right to the grave. No, seriously: release them and let them go. You must also know that just because we forgive someone and release offense, that doesn't mean the relationship is going to be as it was before. There are certain things we do in relationships that make those relationships impossible to be the same ever again. Certain things happen in marriages, and if we don't work through and deal with those things, we might stay together, but the marriage may never be the same.

Do Not Get Lost in the Process

We must not lose ourselves in whatever we are dealing with, must work through, or whatever we are confronting. At the end of the day, we must not find ourselves lost from who we are. There are too many people in the body of Christ who don't know who they are. They have no self-identity because they live their whole lives based on and controlled by other people's actions. We must learn to live our lives, blessing and helping other people, but not losing ourselves in the process. If we can do that, we have yet to discover the best version of ourselves.

The Offense Tool Sheet

Date: ____________________

Time: ____________________

What did I learn about myself today?

____
____
____
____
____

What did the Holy Spirit say to me today?

____
____
____
____
____

What victory did I gain today?

____
____
____
____
____

What is my goal to be a better me?

____
____

How will I handle not being offended in the future?

How will I handle not offending others?

What are my plans to not participate in others' offense?

Who am I praying for that's offended?

A PERSONAL PRAYER FOR YOU

***

Heavenly Father,

Today, I thank you for your love and care for me. That love and care led me to ask for your help in every area of my life. Today, I need victory in all areas of my life where offense may exist. I ask you to forgive me for any offense I have inflicted upon any person, whether I did it knowingly or unknowingly. I repent for causing them any hurt and harm. I ask you to restore them if my actions have caused them short or long-term wounds. I pray the blessing of the Lord upon them, in Jesus' name.

Father, today, I ask you to grant me the grace to forgive anyone who has offended me, both past and present. I will not harbor any offense in my heart. I will not allow offense to dictate my actions nor my life.

Father, by your strength, I release all individuals from the need to ask for my forgiveness, whether they acknowledge their offense against me or not. Your word says that if I don't forgive, I won't be forgiven. Father, I ask you to bless them in every area of their lives.

Father, today, I declare that by the Holy Spirit, I will recognize offense and will use the power of prayer and your word to ensure that I will not be offended and not offend until Christ is formed in me.

I pray this prayer in the name of the Father, the Son, and the Holy Spirit,

Amen.

Made in the USA
Coppell, TX
05 July 2026

84102237R00075